HOW TO

RELAX

LAURA MILNE

vie

HOW TO RELAX

Copyright © Summersdale Publishers Ltd, 2018

Design by Luci Ward

Illustrations © Shutterstock.com

An Hachette UK Company
www.hachette.co.uk

Vie Books, an imprint of Summersdale Publishers Ltd
Part of Octopus Publishing Group Limited
Carmelite House
50 Victoria Embankment
LONDON
EC4Y 0DZ
UK

www.summersdale.com

Printed and bound in China

ISBN: 978-1-78685-538-1

Substantial discounts on bulk quantities of Summersdale books are available to corporations, professional associations and other organisations. For details contact general enquiries: telephone: +44 (0) 1243 771107 or email: enquiries@summersdale.com.

CONTENTS

Introduction: Why We Need to Relax......................4

Relaxation for Every Day..............................6

The Power of the Mind............................41

A Relaxed Home................................65

Ways to Bring Relaxation into Your Life...............86

A Relaxed Body..129

INTRODUCTION

WHY WE NEED TO RELAX

Whether we're racing to meet deadlines at work, managing a health issue or handling a difficult personal situation, stress is an inevitable part of life. And a certain amount of stress in our lives is necessary. It helps our minds and bodies to prepare for difficult challenges and to react appropriately in a crisis.

When we're under pressure, our bodies go into 'fight or flight' mode, our muscles become tense, our heart rate increases and our breathing quickens. Too much continued stress can seriously affect both our physical and mental well-being. Left unchecked, it can lead to feeling burned out or becoming clinically depressed or anxious.

The good news is that there is something you can do about it – learn to relax. Fully relaxing both the mind and body slows the heart and respiration rate and reduces blood pressure, muscle tension and even oxygen consumption. In the coming pages we will look at different techniques that will enable you to let go of the stresses and strains in your life and reach a state of complete calm where clarity of thought and peace of mind can be achieved.

RELAXATION FOR EVERY DAY

A RELAXING ROUTINE

Relaxation exercises can be a powerful weapon against stress. If you learn to relax your breathing and muscles, then it's likely that your mind will follow. In a similar way, easing stressful thoughts and worries in turn helps the body to fully relax.

There are lots of different techniques you can try in the following pages of this book. Whichever you choose, try to practise it at least a couple of times a week so that it will be effective when you need it most. This takes patience and determination, but persevere – it's worth it. Tell yourself that relaxation works like a muscle – the more you exercise it, the stronger it gets.

BALANCE YOUR BREATH

When you're feeling stressed, your
breathing rate becomes faster, shallower
and higher up in your chest. Deep breathing
allows you to take fuller, slower breaths.
Try this kundalini breathing exercise:

1 Sit up straight and pucker
your lips as if holding a
coin between them.

2

Breathe in for a count of four, hold
the breath for a count of four and
then exhale fully through your nose.

3

Do this for a few minutes and
notice how you feel afterwards.

Sometimes the most important thing in a whole day is the rest we take between two deep breaths.

Etty Hillesum

TAKE CHARGE

Being disorganised or leaving things until
the last minute leads to frustrating or crisis
situations, which are likely to make you feel
stressed. If you establish your priorities by
making a daily or weekly to-do list to help you
plan your time effectively, then you are more
likely to feel relaxed and be able to cope –
especially when unexpected obstacles crop up.

Good order is the foundation of all good things.

Edmund Burke

HAVE SOME 'ME' TIME

Taking time to relax is just as important as working or ticking jobs off on your never-ending to-do list. As a minimum, take short relaxation breaks during your busy day. If you can, schedule time in your day just for yourself so that you can recharge your batteries for all the other things you need to do. Learn what your red flags for stress are and have some me time up your sleeve to counteract these when they appear.

TALK IT OUT

Whether it's a trusted friend, a family member or a professional counsellor, finding someone to talk to about your feelings and worries when you are feeling stressed and stuck in a negative spiral can really help you get things off your chest, which, in turn, will help you relax. The simple act of vocalising your thoughts can help you understand them better and think problems through logically, and may even make your worries seem smaller. Talk to people who can help you put things into perspective and work out practical solutions.

STRESS IS A CHOICE:

so is peace of mind

HAVE A CUPPA

There's nothing more comforting than a nice cup of tea. However, too much caffeine can have an impact on sleep quality – research suggests consuming caffeine after midday can negatively affect your sleep, so save your caffeinated teas and coffees for a morning treat and consider switching to a more calming brew after lunch. The menthol contained in peppermint tea is a natural muscle relaxant, making it a great option to have before bedtime. Camomile and valerian contain flavonoids, which also have a calming effect on the brain.

Relax.

EVERYTHING IS RUNNING RIGHT ON SCHEDULE

LEARN TO SAY 'NO'

It's human nature to want to be seen as obliging, but don't feel that you must take on every request or opportunity that comes your way. Saying 'no' doesn't mean you are self-centred or uncaring; it protects you from over-stretching yourself and can be very empowering.

Today I choose serenity

FOLLOW A WIND-DOWN ROUTINE

What's the first thing you do when you
get home from work after a long, stressful
day? Pour a glass of wine and turn on the
TV? Having a wind-down routine can help
you make the mental switch from work
mode to relaxation. Try to avoid stimulating
things, such as alcohol or looking at bright
screens; instead, try getting changed out of
work clothes into pyjamas, reading a book,
listening to soothing music or having a bath
with some relaxing essential oils, such as
lavender, to help you feel relaxed and sleepy.

There is more to life than increasing its speed.

Mahatma Gandhi

SHAKE IT OFF

Vigorous movement can help to relax our bodies and get them ready for sleep, as it tires out the muscles and helps relieve tension. That doesn't mean you need to head to the gym – try jumping up and down or running on the spot, imagining that you are shaking the energy out of your system, and you will be ready for bed in no time. If you find this too stimulating before bed, try doing it earlier in the afternoon instead of in the evening.

DO A BODY SCAN

Stress not only affects our emotions but can manifest itself as physical symptoms. Tension in the jaw or neck, digestive problems and headaches can all result from stress. If you learn to recognise these signs in your own body, you have a chance to deal with the problem before it gets too out of hand.

A key way of checking this mind-body connection is to give yourself a 'body scan'. Sit quietly and systematically assess your body, starting at the top of your head and moving down over your face, the back of your head, your shoulders,

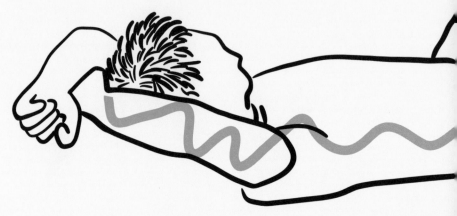

arms, hands, torso, hips, legs and feet. As you do this, notice the sensations you feel. Are there any areas of tension, pressure or discomfort? If so, breathe into these areas and allow them to soften and relax.

Practising this technique on a regular basis can help you become more alert to the messages your body is sending. By exploring the link between body and mind, you will start to notice which parts of the body become tense or out of balance when you experience a particular emotion, and can take steps to alleviate the tension.

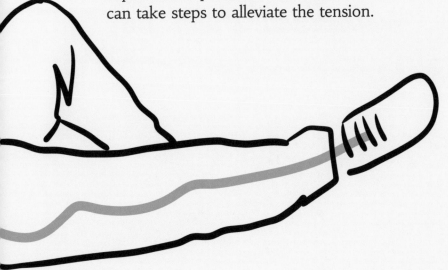

Each of us needs to withdraw from the cares which will not withdraw from us.

Maya Angelou

HUG SOMEONE YOU LOVE

Our worries melt away when we are in a hug. This is because having a cuddle releases the hormone oxytocin from the brain, which causes muscles to relax and releases tension in the body. It elevates mood and alleviates stress by reducing the levels of circulating stress hormone cortisol, and calming the mind.

A CHANGE IS AS GOOD

as a rest

PRACTISE YOGA

Yoga is an ancient discipline that combines physical poses, controlled breathing and meditation. Studies have found that regular practice can help reduce stress, lower blood pressure and heart rate.

Although there are many different styles of yoga, Hatha yoga may be a good choice for stress management, and beginners often find the slower pace easier to follow.

The British Wheel of Yoga (www.bwy.org.uk) is a good place to look for a class with a qualified teacher in your local area. There are also lots of classes available online. Search on YouTube for free tutorials.

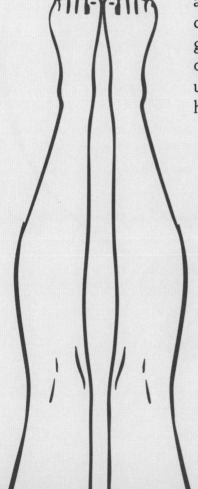

PUT YOUR FEET UP

The Vipariti Kirani yoga pose, which is suitable for beginners, involves lying on the floor and resting your legs up against a wall for a few minutes (shuffle your bottom as close to the wall as you can). This relaxing pose will give the body a good stretch out after a day spent crunched up in an office chair. It also helps create peace of mind.

Slow down;
there's no
need to rush

TUNE IN TO THE MUSIC

Listening to the right music has the
power to take away all your worries.
When you're feeling stressed, belting
out your favourite song can give you
an energy boost; alternatively, classical
music can be especially relaxing right
before bedtime. Create a playlist of
your favourite stress-busting tracks and
listen to it whenever you feel the need.

FLOW WITH WHATEVER MAY HAPPEN AND LET YOUR MIND BE FREE: STAY CENTRED BY ACCEPTING WHATEVER YOU ARE DOING.

Zhuang Zhou

SHRUG IT OFF

A quick way of relaxing
your shoulder and neck
muscles if you have been
sitting at your desk for a
long time is to simply shrug
your shoulders by raising
them to your ears and then
relaxing them. Repeat a
few times to release tension
whenever you feel stressed.

Take a deep breath
and let things go

TAKE A QUICK POWER WALK

When you're feeling overwhelmed
or having trouble concentrating,
go for a quick stroll around the
block. You'll get the benefits of
alone time and physical activity as
well as a few minutes to gather
your thoughts and de-stress.

It does good also to take walks out of doors, that our spirits may be raised and refreshed by the open air and fresh breeze.

Seneca

EMERGENCY CALM

If you are feeling extremely anxious and need to control your body's stress response, you can 'reset' yourself by applying pressure to a point between your second and third knuckles. Move your thumb down your middle finger toward your palm. You will be able to feel a soft, slightly indented spot on the inside of your finger if your palm is facing up. Apply medium pressure to this spot on either hand for a few minutes to restore your equilibrium.

THE POWER OF THE MIND

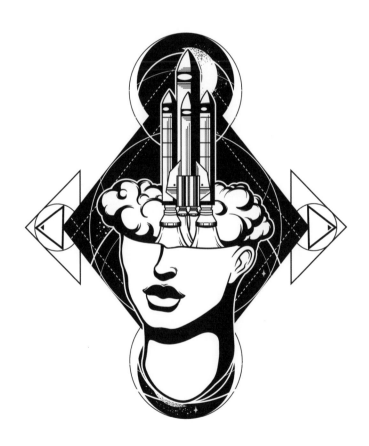

WHAT'S STOPPING YOU
FROM RELAXING?

We all have a tendency towards certain
negative thought patterns. Start paying
attention to these types of thoughts to help
you work out what is preventing you from
achieving peace of mind. Do you tend to dwell
on the past? Or are you filled with worry
about what may happen in the future? Do you
ruminate on petty arguments you've had or
hold grudges against others who you feel have
wronged you? Writing these tendencies down
can help you to identify the mental obstacles
that may be stopping you from fully relaxing.

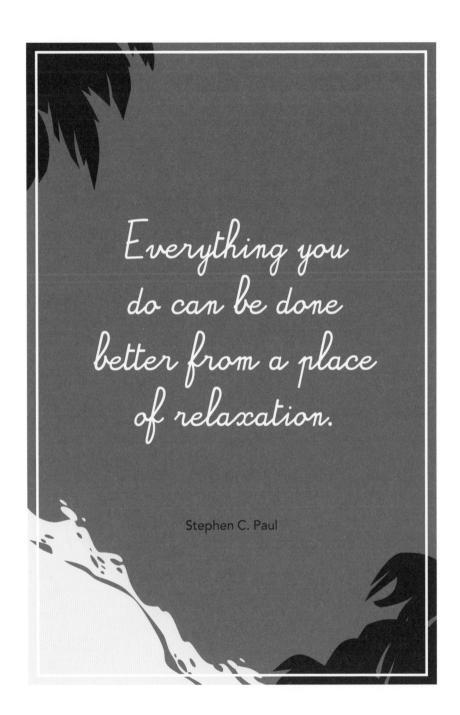

Everything you
do can be done
better from a place
of relaxation.

Stephen C. Paul

Have you ever noticed that some people can become stressed out about a situation that others don't seem to be bothered by?

If you perceive a situation or event as being dangerous, difficult or painful, then you are more likely to feel tense about it before you've even started, whether your perception is accurate or not. Try to focus less on how awful you think something is going to be and more on practical ways of handling it, and see how your experience changes with a proactive mindset.

Life isn't as serious
as your mind makes
it out to be.

Eckhart Tolle

SAY OMM

Meditation is a kind of mental exercise that can involve concentrating on your breath or repeating a mantra. Well-known types of meditation include Transcendental Meditation (TM), prayer, Zen meditation, Taoist meditation, mindfulness meditation and Buddhist meditation. Whichever the style, the goal is the same: a mind that is quiet and free from stress. Experiment with a few different types to find out if one of them works for you.

It's a good idea
always to do something
relaxing prior to
making an important
decision in your life.

Paulo Coelho

BE MINDFUL

Mindfulness is a thought process derived from Buddhist teachings. It's simply about focusing on the present moment. Rather than fretting about the past or worrying about the future, the aim is to fully experience life as it unfolds.

Practised regularly, this simple technique can be immensely powerful. It encourages us to stop constantly striving for something new or better and become more balanced and grounded instead.

A few moments of mindfulness every day could allow you to find more peace and relaxation in your life.

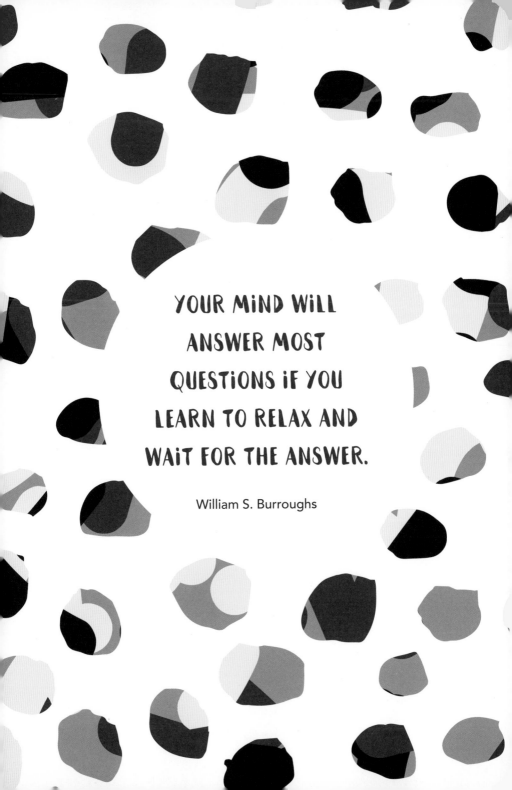

YOUR MIND WILL
ANSWER MOST
QUESTIONS IF YOU
LEARN TO RELAX AND
WAIT FOR THE ANSWER.

William S. Burroughs

MAKE TEATIME A MINDFUL MOMENT

Many of us go through our daily routines on autopilot, barely noticing what we're doing. An easy way to focus your attention on the present is to concentrate all your attention on simple tasks. For example, when you are making a cup of tea, pay attention to the sound of the water heating in the kettle and the wisps of steam coming from the spout; as you pour the water, watch the colour of the water change as it hits the teabag; listen to the gurgling of the liquid as it fills the cup. As you stir your drink, listen to the clink of the teaspoon against the cup; as you take a sip, feel the mug warm your fingers; then, rather than gulping it down, savour the taste and notice any thoughts that arise.

Whenever your mind wanders into negative thoughts, gently return your attention to what you are doing.

TAKE A BREAK

Humans are only wired to be able to focus on
a single task for an hour or two at most, before
our minds become fatigued and begin to wander.
Alpha brain waves, which are present when our
minds are relaxed, are responsible for processing
and storing all the new information the brain has
taken in and making new connections that spark
creativity. That's why we have our best ideas in
the bath or when we're making a cup of tea –
because our brains are taking a mental rest.

Taking a break doesn't have to take up lots of time either. Stepping away from stressful situations for a few minutes or taking time away from your normal routines and thoughts can give you enough space and distance to feel calmer. Reading a book or flipping through a magazine, even if it's only for a few minutes, or taking a quick stroll around the block, should be enough to reset yourself.

THINK HAPPY THOUGHTS

Visualisation can be a very useful means of achieving mindfulness. This method involves breathing deeply while focusing on pleasant, positive images rather than letting your mind automatically drift into negative thought patterns. If you are feeling anxious or exhausted, try this simple practice: close your eyes and visualise a hot-air balloon. Imagine you are putting all your stress and worries into the balloon. Then watch it gently rise up and float away into the distance, taking your troubles with it.

LIFE IS 10 PER CENT WHAT HAPPENS TO YOU AND 90 PER CENT HOW YOU REACT TO IT.

Charles R. Swindoll

THINK POSITIVELY

Try to find other ways of thinking
about stressful situations and
talk to yourself in a positive way.
For example, say to yourself: 'I
can handle this', 'This will all
be over soon' or 'I've faced this
before and I can do it again.'

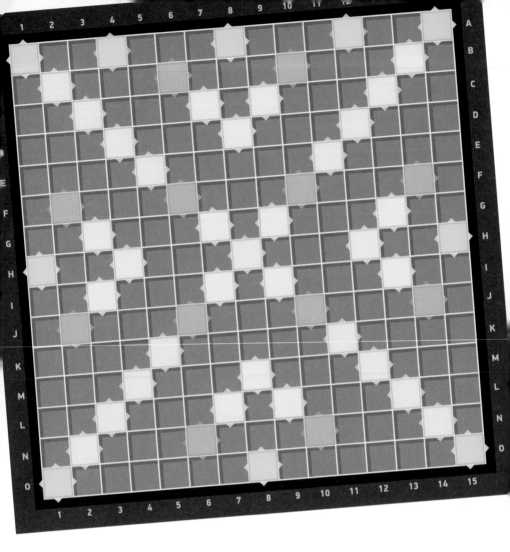

PLAY A BRAIN GAME

If you're feeling anxious or overwhelmed, play a few brain games that require a certain amount of concentration: crossword puzzles, Sudoku or Scrabble can help take your mind off whatever is worrying you, as your brain can only be actively engaged in one task at a time.

STOP MULTI-TASKING

We pride ourselves on our ability to be able to do a number of things at once, but in reality, when our brains are rapidly switching back and forth between tasks, such as when we take a phone call while continuing to work on a document on the computer, what's really happening is that one of the two activities is carried out on autopilot. It also takes several seconds to get your brain into each 'mode' required for the different activities, meaning we're actually less productive when multi-tasking, not more, and we waste time every time we switch between jobs. Your mind can become distracted and agitated as result.

So, rather than saving time, trying to do several things at once actually takes longer. Instead of multi-tasking, try doing one thing at a time and give your full attention to it. When you've finished, move on to the next task and so on. Notice how much calmer and more relaxed you feel when you're not distracted and can focus on one thing at a time.

Set peace of
mind as your
highest goal,
and organise
your life
around it.

Brian Tracy

REMEMBER: YOU DON'T HAVE TO BE PERFECT

Continually striving for perfection, which in itself is an impossible goal, is exhausting. If you are constantly comparing yourself to someone who you think has a better job, a bigger house or more money than you, you are likely to feel tense and discontented with your lot in life.

Rest satisfied with
doing well and leave
others to talk of you
as they please.

Pythagoras

A RELAXED HOME

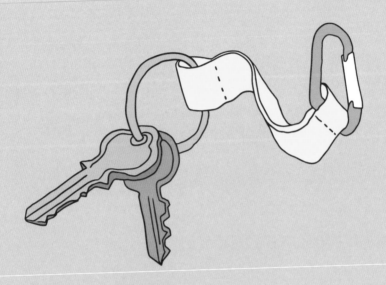

CLEAR YOUR CLUTTER

Living in a tidy, clutter-free environment can have a big impact on your stress levels. Think about the last time you were late because you couldn't find your car keys or a clean shirt. Having a place for everything is calming, and being able to locate things you need quickly means that you are less likely to be in a rush. Decluttering your entire house or flat in one go might appear to be an overwhelming task but breaking it down into smaller, more manageable sessions will make it less daunting. Dedicating just 10 minutes a day to getting rid of items that you no longer find useful, or that no longer give you any pleasure, can be immensely satisfying and calming.

TIDY HOUSE, TIDY MIND

PAINT YOUR ROOMS BLUE

The colours we choose to decorate our surroundings with can have a huge impact on our mental well-being. Red shades tend to trigger the body's stress response, making us more anxious, while lighter, cooler shades calm us down. Blue is thought to be a soothing colour that helps calm the mind, slow the heart rate, lower blood pressure and reduce anxiety.

FIND YOUR

YOUR

OFF

SWITCH

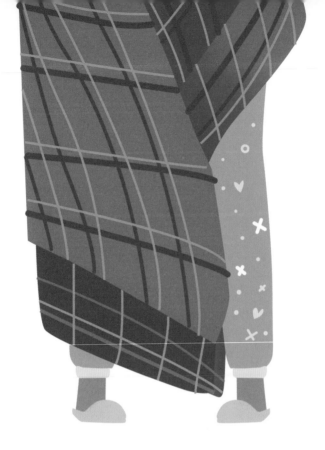

HAVE A PYJAMA DAY

Spending the whole day in your
pyjamas might not be something
you choose to do very often, but
occasionally it can be intensely
relaxing. Having a whole day dedicated
to resting and doing whatever you
like, such as reading or watching
movies, can be very restorative. The
only rule is: you are only allowed
to do things that you enjoy.

BAKE A CAKE

From weighing out the flour, sugar and butter to beating the mixture and enjoying the end results afterwards, baking has a calming, meditative quality that can help to ease anxiety. And if you're baking bread, the simple repetitive action of kneading the dough can be especially soothing, creating space for thoughts to come and go. The aroma of baking bread is one of the most comforting smells there is, and the sense of satisfaction you get from creating something that looks and tastes delicious can be huge.

If you do what you Love, it is the best way to relax.

Christian Louboutin

CREATE A SLEEP SANCTUARY

The more calm and peaceful your bedroom is, the more likely you are to view it as an inviting place that you associate with restfulness and sleep. Experts recommend keeping your bedroom cool, dark, clean and clutter-free. Remove all items to do with work or study, including electronics such as TVs or smartphones. Invest in a high-quality mattress and comfortable bedding that will make you look forward to bedtime. Soothing scents such as lavender and jasmine help create a calming atmosphere.

CLEAN IT UP

If you've had a stressful day, sometimes the best thing you can do is roll up your sleeves and get scrubbing. The act of cleaning your home, if done properly, has the added benefit of giving you a good workout, which can be great for relieving stress.

Running up and down stairs, carrying things from room to room and scrubbing windows or floors can burn calories, release endorphins and help you blow off steam – especially if you put on some upbeat music while you work. And at the end of it, you get the satisfaction and enjoyment of having a clean and tidy living space in which to relax.

NOURISHING THE SOUL WILL INSPIRE DREAMS

LET AN OPEN FIRE CALM YOU

Sitting by a cosy log fire when it's cold and wet outside is the perfect antidote to those dark winter evenings. Now studies have even shown that watching the crackling flames and flickering light causes blood pressure to drop and leaves us feeling more at ease.

The relaxing effect is believed to be evolutionary, harking back to prehistoric times, when Stone Age man socialised around camp fires, feeling safe and warm while bonding with friends. If you haven't got an open hearth, downloading a video of a crackling fire as the screensaver on your smart TV or computer can induce a similar effect.

GET OUT IN THE GARDEN

Planting, pruning, raking
leaves or even just pulling
out weeds can restore
your equilibrium after
a busy or stressful day.
When the weather is
warm enough, going
barefoot and feeling
the grass beneath
your feet will
heighten the
experience.

PLANT A 'GOOD MOOD' HERB GARDEN

Getting your hands dirty in the garden is great for combating stress. Even if you don't have access to your own green space, you can still plant your own 'good mood' garden of edible herbs in pots or containers, which can be kept on a balcony or kitchen windowsill.

Oregano, for example, is rich in caffeic acid, quercetin and rosmarinic acid, all components that combat fatigue and anxiety, and what's more, as with most herbs, oregano is easy to grow. Seedlings can be bought at a local nursery or supermarket, then potted and watered as needed.

It is nice finding that place where you can just go and relax.

Moisés Arias

LUXURIATE IN A HOT BATH

A warm bath can help increase blood flow and reduce stiffness and pain in joints and muscles – and less pain equals a more relaxed body and mind. It is the perfect place to let your mind wander and appreciate the soothing feeling of the warm water against your skin. Light a candle and enjoy watching the flickering shadows dance against the wall and reflections in the water. For an extra bubbly bath, add two mugs of sodium bicarbonate and immerse yourself for 20 glorious minutes.

THERE MUST BE
QUITE A FEW
THINGS THAT
A HOT BATH
WON'T CURE,
BUT I DON'T
KNOW MANY
OF THEM.

Sylvia Plath

IF YOU HAVE A GARDEN AND A LIBRARY, YOU HAVE EVERYTHING YOU NEED.

Cicero

SOOTHING SCENTS

Sprinkle a few drops of lavender, tea tree, or another essential oil into your palms or on your pillow and inhale. These soothing scents reduce stress and anxiety by stimulating smell receptors in the nose that connect to the part of the brain that regulates emotions. Keeping a scented candle or reed diffuser on your bedside table can also help send you off to sleep.

WAYS TO BRING RELAXATION INTO YOUR LIFE

TAKE
TIME TO
DO WHAT
MAKES
YOUR SOUL
HAPPY

DO NOTHING

We often assume that the way to get more done is to push ourselves, or others, to keep going for longer. But our brains depend on downtime – not just for recharging batteries, but to process the vast amount of information that we are deluged with every day. Periods of doing nothing – or very little – are vital in order to consolidate memory and reinforce learning by strengthening the brain's neural pathways.

Whether you lie on the bed and stare at the ceiling or gaze out the window, don't expect doing nothing to feel easy at first. Resisting the urge to check your phone for messages, tidy up or get on with your to-do list takes willpower. But learning to do nothing – even if it's just for a few minutes every day – will help you take back control of your attention at other times.

Rest and inactivity also allow insights and inspiration to flow. It's when we're in this state of just 'being' that ideas or solutions to problems that we have been wrestling with suddenly come to us.

I have what I call 'should-less'
days. Today is a day where
there is nothing I 'should' do.

Ellen Burstyn

WRITE IT DOWN

Setting your worries down on paper can be highly cathartic. Buy yourself a beautiful journal that you'll want to write in, or, if you prefer, a cheap notebook that you don't mind scribbling in, and start writing. Write about what's on your mind and what has been bothering you lately. If you have a stressful event coming up, putting your fears about it on paper can make it seem less intimidating.

VISIT A CHURCH

Ancient temples and churches
can bring a sense of peace
to a troubled mind. Most
historic places of worship
were designed to fill visitors
with a sense of relaxation,
grounding and inner peace.

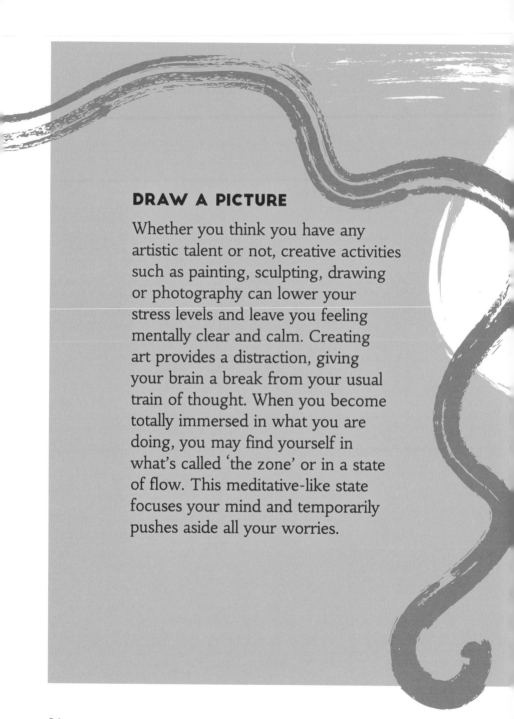

DRAW A PICTURE

Whether you think you have any artistic talent or not, creative activities such as painting, sculpting, drawing or photography can lower your stress levels and leave you feeling mentally clear and calm. Creating art provides a distraction, giving your brain a break from your usual train of thought. When you become totally immersed in what you are doing, you may find yourself in what's called 'the zone' or in a state of flow. This meditative-like state focuses your mind and temporarily pushes aside all your worries.

TAKE A SOUND BATH

Sound bathing, which has been around for thousands of years, involves listening to sounds generated by singing bowls, gongs, bells and other instruments. The vibrations generated by the sounds induce a meditative state which leads to intense relaxation, a reduction of stress and pain, a lower heart rate and less anxiety. This alternative therapy is becoming increasingly popular and is often offered in yoga or wellness centres. Try searching 'sound bath' or 'gong bath' on Google to find out whether it is available near you.

Take rest; a field
that is rested gives
a bountiful crop.

Ovid

GIVE YOURSELF A DIGITAL DETOX

The constant stream of information and data we receive from mobiles, computers and TV can be overwhelming, and research has shown that the urge many of us have to keep checking for updates leaves us feeling irritable, anxious and unable to concentrate. So it's a good idea to give yourself regular breaks. Turn off all your devices for an hour or two every day for some respite from the barrage of emails, texts and social media notifications.

PLAY WITH A PET

Having a dog or cat around comes with many benefits. Research has revealed that simply spending time with their pet leaves owners feeling more relaxed, more optimistic and less preoccupied with everyday worries.

Taking a dog for a walk has been shown to be a profound and effective stress reducer, increasing feelings of contentment and relaxation. If you don't own a pet, sites such as borrowmydoggy.com connect you with local dog owners who are happy to let you take their pooch for a walk, or you could offer dog-walking services to friends or family members with pets.

Who among us hasn't envied a cat's ability to ignore the cares of daily life and to relax completely?

Karen Brademeyer

WATCH THE CLOUDS

If you want an instant hit of relaxation, lie on the grass and spend a few moments just watching the clouds drift by. Do they resemble objects, animals or people that you know? This exercise can be similar to mindful meditation – you are just watching clouds go by, instead of your thoughts.

OUR MIND IS LIKE A
BLUE SKY. CLOUDS
COME AND GO. WE
TEND TO GET CAUGHT
UP IN THE CLOUDS
AND FORGET ABOUT
THE BLUE SKY.

Andy Puddicombe

GAZE AT THE STARS

Many of us never take the time to look up at the night sky, but the vast expanse above can do much to calm your soul. When our attention is solely focused on day-to-day problems or to-do lists, we tend to forget that we are living on a tiny planet on the edge of our galaxy. But go outside at night and look up in wonder at the infinite number of stars in the night sky and you get a sense of how small and insignificant we are in the universe. This feeling of awe steers our focus away from our problems and relaxes a weary mind.

LISTEN TO A BEDTIME STORY

Think back to when you were a child, and how much you enjoyed listening to bedtime stories. It was comforting, relaxing and put you in just the right frame of mind to drift off to sleep.

There's no reason that, just because you're an adult now, you can't still benefit from being read to, to help you unwind. Apps such as Calm (calm.com) contain sleep stories for adults that let your brain relax and prepare for a deep rest, just as they did when you were young, or you could download a calming audiobook and set the sleep timer so you can drift off as you're being read to.

FIND A
PLACE TO

calm
your mind

& RECHARGE
YOUR SOUL

LISTEN TO THE OCEAN

The hypnotic sound of ocean waves gently
lapping against the shore has to be one
of the most calming sounds in the world
and can even help you nod off to sleep.
It's partly because the brain interprets this
and other rhythmic soundtracks, such as
pattering raindrops in a quiet forest or the
low rumble of a distant thunderstorm, as
'non-threats' and can use them to block out
other, more alarming or unpleasant noises.
If you don't live near the real thing, try
searching on YouTube for 'calming ocean
waves sounds' to find a recording, and see
if it has a relaxing effect on your mood.

TAKE AN EARLY MORNING STROLL

Go for a mindful walk early in the morning when the air is fresh and crisp. Listen to the birds and watch the sun rise. Be mindful of each step you take, as well as fully appreciating the sights, sounds and smells. Start your morning in a calm and restful way, and the rest of the day should follow suit – and you will be better prepared to tackle whatever the day throws at you.

An early morning walk is a blessing for the whole day.

Henry David Thoreau

GO ON A SILENT RETREAT

By introducing moments of peace and quiet into your everyday life, you can help achieve balance and give yourself the space you need to allow your mind and body to relax. This is something you can do in small moments on your own, but why not step it up a notch by going on a silent retreat? Retreat centres offer the chance of committing to a period of silence for a few days or even longer. During a silent retreat you agree to cut all contact with the outside world, and stays often include meditation or yoga sessions. Going on a meditation retreat can be profoundly relaxing because it provides the opportunity to experience the benefits of silence in an intense way.

HAVE A GOSSIP

Most of us don't need an excuse for getting together with friends for a chat, but research shows a good gossip boosts levels of endorphins, the hormones that reduce anxiety and stress.

Conversation also plays an important part in social bonding, making us happier and more relaxed.

PLAY CHILDHOOD GAMES

Jump on a trampoline, go roller-skating, play hopscotch, try hula hooping, find a skipping rope or blow bubbles. Going back to your childhood and rediscovering how to play your favourite games is a great stress-buster and will put you in a happier, more carefree mindset.

Think a little less, Live a little More

THERE IS VIRTUE IN WORK AND THERE IS VIRTUE IN REST. USE BOTH AND OVERLOOK NEITHER.

Alan Cohen

DANCE IT OFF

Humans have probably been dancing since the beginning of time, and most cultures on earth enjoy some form of rhythmic movement to music. But why is it that such a simple act has the ability to lift our spirits? Scientists believe we get a much bigger release of endorphins when we dance than during any other form of exercise. Dancing connects with the emotional centres in the brain, which is why, for many of us, it gives us a feeling of uncomplicated happiness or allows us to release pent-up emotions. You don't have to be an accomplished ballroom dancer to get the benefits either. Just put on your favourite music and go for it!

The time to relax

IS WHEN YOU DON'T HAVE TIME FOR IT.

Sydney J. Harris

GET LOST IN A GOOD BOOK

Reading is one of the best ways to relax, and even a few minutes can be enough to reduce your stress levels. Researchers believe it's because the human mind has to concentrate on reading and the distraction of being taken into a fictional world eases muscle tension.

Your choice of reading material really doesn't matter; it is the act of losing yourself in a thoroughly engrossing book that allows you to escape from the worries and stresses of your everyday world. Using your imagination to actively engage with the words on the printed page stimulates your creativity and causes you to enter an altered state of consciousness, which is profoundly relaxing.

Find your own
path to relaxation

and follow it

CLEAR OUT YOUR INBOX

Have you ever considered how the constant stream of information and data you are subjected to daily affects your ability to relax? Even the act of quickly scanning an email requires your brain to make several decisions: whether or not to click on a link within it, delete the email or reply to it. The sheer volume of data we receive on a daily basis forces our brains to subconsciously make hundreds of these micro decisions every day. It is not only mentally exhausting but makes it difficult for our brains to switch off. Reduce this information overload by blocking junk mail, unsubscribing from online magazine subscriptions that you never have time to read and removing other email alerts that clutter up your inbox. You may be surprised at just how calm a clear inbox makes you feel.

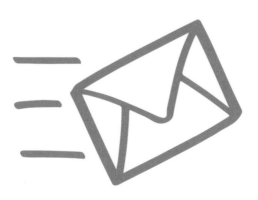

TRY CREATIVE WELL-BEING ACTIVITIES

Creative activities, such as colouring-in, crochet and origami, are thought to promote relaxation and sleep. Grab some felt tips and an adult colouring book before you go to bed as part of your wind-down routine – 20 minutes or so can help you relax and drift off to sleep.

Find your Flow

SLIME TIME

It might sound baffling at first, but people rave about how relaxed they feel after playing with homemade slime – a gloopy substance you can poke, prod, stretch, fold or just play around with to alleviate stress.

To make your own slime, pour a small bottle of PVA glue into a bowl, add some food colouring and mix. Make it fluffy with a few pumps of shaving foam or soap (the foaming kind in a bottle with a dispenser) and mix, and add a few drops of contact lens solution at a time. Knead it between your hands. It will start off sticking to them but in about 20 seconds the slime will firm up, becoming elastic and stretchy. Think of it as an extra-fun, extra-stress-busting stress ball!

LEARNING TO IGNORE THINGS
IS ONE OF THE GREAT
PATHS TO INNER PEACE.

Robert J. Sawyer

HAVE A GIGGLE

Laughter is a powerful antidote to stress, pain and anxiety. Nothing works faster or more dependably to bring your mind and body back into balance. A good, hearty laugh relieves physical tension and stress, leaving your muscles relaxed for up to 45 minutes. The reason that TV sitcoms use canned laughter is because it's contagious. You're more likely to laugh when you hear other people laughing. The more laughter you bring into your life, the happier and more relaxed you are likely to feel. Watching your favourite comedy show, funny film or YouTube video can be a great way to get your hit of humour for the day.

A GOOD
LAUGH SETS
EVERYTHING
STRAIGHT

A RELAXED BODY

TAKE CARE OF YOUR BODY

When we feel overwhelmed we tend to eat poorly,
sleep less, stop exercising and generally push
ourselves harder. This can overtax the immune
system, causing us to fall ill more easily.

If you take good care of yourself to begin with
– by eating regular meals, including plenty
of fresh fruit and vegetables, wholegrains
and lean sources of protein such as nuts and
pulses, keeping active, getting regular rest
and doing things you enjoy – you'll be better
prepared to manage stress in the long run.

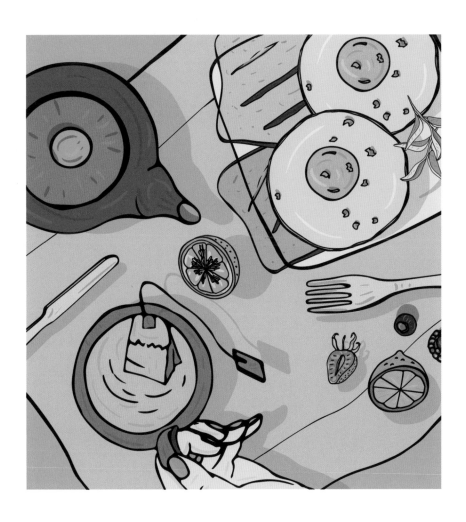

One cannot think well, love well,
sleep well, if one has not dined well.

Virginia Woolf

EXERCISE REGULARLY

Whether it's a jog around the
park or a pumping spin class,
any kind of regular workout
that elevates your heart rate
and gets your body moving is a
great way of relieving stress and
tension. It causes the body to
release endorphins, the mood-
elevating hormones, and reduces
levels of stress hormones such as
adrenaline and cortisol. Exercise
is also a way of taking time out
for yourself, as well as building
confidence and self-esteem.

EAT SLOWLY

Wolfing down your food without really tasting it or taking the time to chew each mouthful properly plays havoc with your digestive system and can lead to overeating. As you eat your meal, focus all your attention on the smell, taste and texture of the food you are eating. Putting down your fork between mouthfuls allows you time to appreciate the food you are eating and consider whether you are still hungry or if you are just clearing your plate for the sake of it. Eating mindfully means that you are more likely to finish a meal feeling relaxed and satisfied.

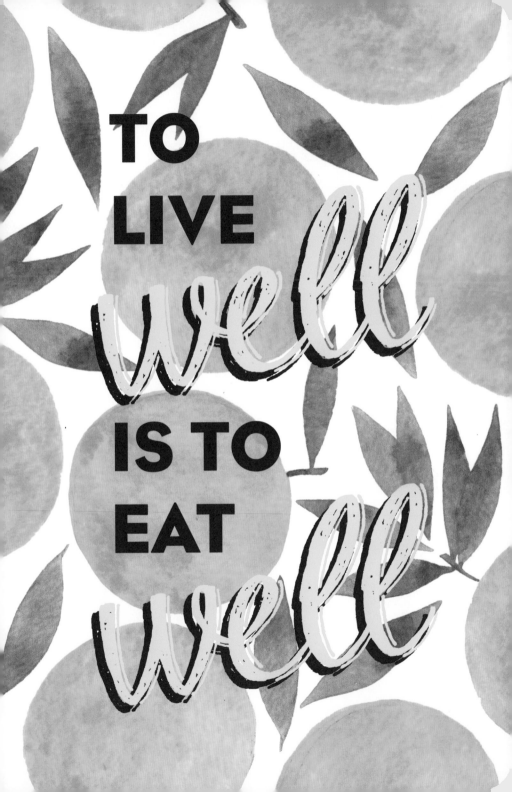

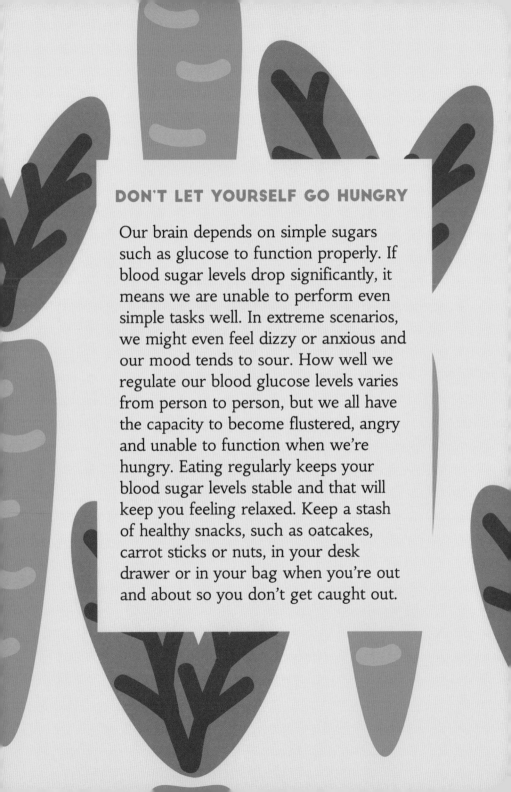

DON'T LET YOURSELF GO HUNGRY

Our brain depends on simple sugars such as glucose to function properly. If blood sugar levels drop significantly, it means we are unable to perform even simple tasks well. In extreme scenarios, we might even feel dizzy or anxious and our mood tends to sour. How well we regulate our blood glucose levels varies from person to person, but we all have the capacity to become flustered, angry and unable to function when we're hungry. Eating regularly keeps your blood sugar levels stable and that will keep you feeling relaxed. Keep a stash of healthy snacks, such as oatcakes, carrot sticks or nuts, in your desk drawer or in your bag when you're out and about so you don't get caught out.

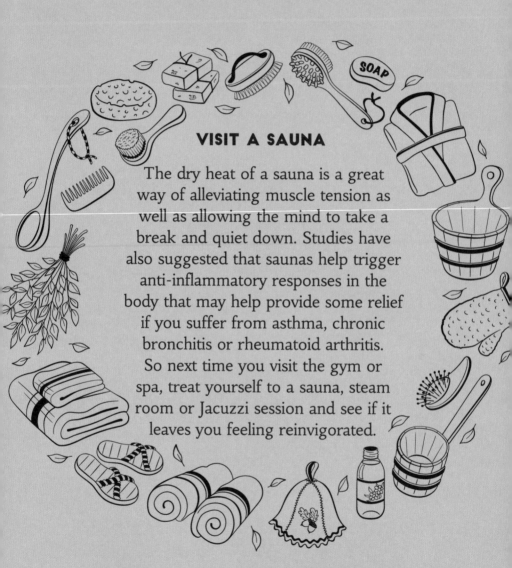

VISIT A SAUNA

The dry heat of a sauna is a great way of alleviating muscle tension as well as allowing the mind to take a break and quiet down. Studies have also suggested that saunas help trigger anti-inflammatory responses in the body that may help provide some relief if you suffer from asthma, chronic bronchitis or rheumatoid arthritis. So next time you visit the gym or spa, treat yourself to a sauna, steam room or Jacuzzi session and see if it leaves you feeling reinvigorated.

BLOW UP A BALLOON

It might feel a bit silly at first, but when extreme stress hits, inflating a balloon could be a clever way of tricking your body into breathing deeply. Your body needs oxygen to relax, and when you're under pressure you're likely to take shorter, shallower breaths. Blowing up a balloon forces you to breathe more slowly and deeply since you're using your diaphragm. It also activates your parasympathetic nervous system, reducing your heart rate and relaxing your muscles. Keep a few balloons handy in case of emergencies!

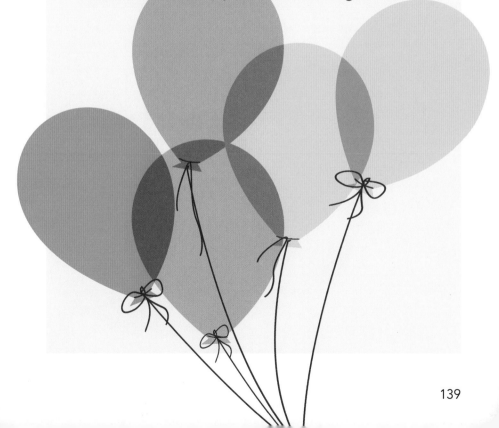

LET YOUR WORRIES FLOAT AWAY

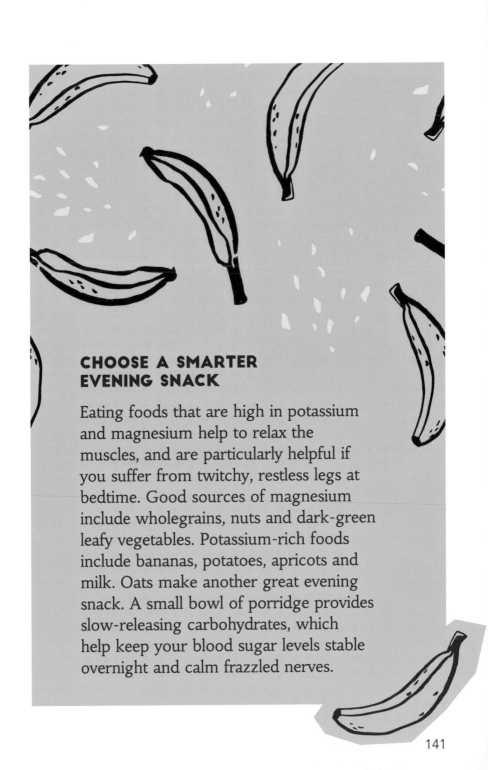

CHOOSE A SMARTER EVENING SNACK

Eating foods that are high in potassium and magnesium help to relax the muscles, and are particularly helpful if you suffer from twitchy, restless legs at bedtime. Good sources of magnesium include wholegrains, nuts and dark-green leafy vegetables. Potassium-rich foods include bananas, potatoes, apricots and milk. Oats make another great evening snack. A small bowl of porridge provides slow-releasing carbohydrates, which help keep your blood sugar levels stable overnight and calm frazzled nerves.

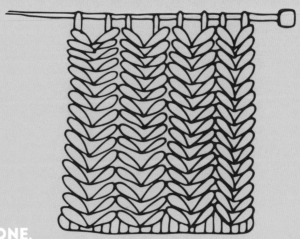

KNIT ONE,
PURL ONE

When you pick up a pair of knitting needles and cast on, you are, without even realising it, taking part in a form of meditation. Research has shown that listening to the quiet click of the needles along with the rhythmic and repetitive action of making the stitches induces the 'relaxation response' in a similar way to that of yoga or progressive muscle relaxation (see p.144).

On top of that, knitting can lower the heart rate by an average of 11 beats per minute, as well as reducing blood pressure and muscle tension.

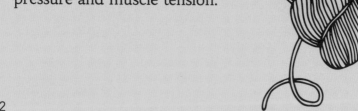

All that is harmony for you, my Universe, is in harmony with me as well.

Marcus Aurelius

TENSE AND RELAX

Progressive muscle relaxation (PMR) is a relaxation technique that involves sequentially tensing and relaxing different muscle groups, starting with your toes and working your way up your body. Hold the tension for 5 seconds and then slowly relax your muscles. Researchers think this technique may help boost awareness of the physical sensations associated with relaxation, training your body so it knows how to relax the muscles more easily in future.

Find meaning in
every moment

TRY A SELF-MASSAGE

A good massage can not only help you relax but also help alleviate anxiety, headaches, sleep issues and sore, tight muscles. If you can't book into a spa for a treatment, you can give yourself a very effective self-massage. Abhyanga is an Ayurvedic practice that can be highly relaxing.

To try it yourself, heat some massage oil in the microwave or on the stove until it's warm but still comfortable to touch. Massage your body with the oil, moving from the head to the feet. Begin with the outer folds of your ears, then massage your head and neck and work downwards. Use gentle circular motions on the joints and over the heart and abdomen. Massage straight up and down on the arms and legs. Finally, thoroughly massage your feet. Lie down and relax for at least 10 minutes, allowing the oil to penetrate your skin. When you are finished, remove the oil using a gentle cleanser.

ADD A PINCH OF NUTMEG

Nutmeg has been used in folk medicine for centuries to relieve anxiety and for its sleep-inducing properties. A little goes a long way, so don't overdo it. Add a pinch of nutmeg to a glass of warm milk or sprinkle a little onto some slices of banana before you go to bed. Add some cardamom for added benefits.

HAVE A GOOD CRY

When it all gets to be too much,
go ahead and let the tears fall.
Studies have shown that having a
good weep helps release pent-up
emotions. You might be surprised
by just how cathartic it is to allow
yourself to let go of tension you've
been bottling up all day. You
may feel emotionally fragile and
drained for a while afterwards, so
be kind to yourself. Splash some
cold water on your face to soothe
blotchy skin and make yourself
a warm, comforting drink.

There
can be
no peace
without,

but
through
peace
within.

William Ellery Channing

TAKE A DIP

A regular evening swim might
keep you fit but it's the rhythmic
strokes and the sound of
the lapping water that make
swimming so much more
relaxing than other types of
exercise. It produces the same
relaxation response as yoga. All
you have to focus on is your
strokes and breathing, dissolving
those negative thoughts.

HUG A HOT-WATER BOTTLE

The humble hot-water bottle has been used for generations to aid relaxation and relieve aches and pains – and with good reason. If your hands and feet are cold in bed you are more likely to suffer from restlessness and insomnia. Sleep researchers have found that putting a hot-water bottle at your feet switches on the body's sleep mechanism, and it can also ease stress and tension in the body. Try lying on your back with a hot-water bottle under your neck to relax aching shoulder and neck muscles, or on your stomach to soothe and comfort you as you drift off to sleep. Just remember not to use boiling water and to check the seal before you get into bed with it!

GET CHEWING

If you know you're heading into a stressful situation, try chewing a piece of gum. Studies have found that chewing gum can help lower cortisol levels and help you relax. It can also keep you from snacking in between meals and overeating, which is a negative side effect of stress – win-win!

TAKE A NAP

Research has shown that a short daily siesta can not only improve your mood and give you an energy boost for the afternoon, but it can even reduce the risk of heart attack. If curling up in your office isn't an option, go somewhere quiet on your break, such as a church or a park bench, and close your eyes for just a few minutes to reap the same benefits.

WHEN IT'S TIME TO SEE YOUR GP

If you are still struggling to relax despite trying some of the strategies in this book, and feel that stress is having a negative effect on your day-to-day life, it may be worth seeing your doctor.

Although self-help measures and complementary therapies can be helpful tools for coping with everyday pressures, some situations require medical advice.

Asking for help is nothing to be ashamed of: remember your doctor is there to help, not to judge you. Your GP may recommend a talking therapy such as CBT (cognitive behavioural therapy) or medication. Try to be honest with your doctor and give as much detail as possible about how you are feeling and what you've already tried. That way, they will have all the information they need to give you the best possible advice and treatment.

IMAGE CREDITS

If you're interested in finding out more
about our books, find us on Facebook
at Summersdale Publishers and follow
us on Twitter at @Summersdale.

WWW.SUMMERSDALE.COM